To Change or Not To Change

Your Choice Will Make You Bitter or Better

by Dr. M. Duane Rawlins

Other Books by
Dr. M. Duane Rawlins

More Than a Father

Raising Kids Right in a World Gone Wrong

God, Is This Your Final Answer?

God, If This is Your Final Anwer,
How Shall We Live?

God, If This is Your Final Anwer,
How Shall We Give?

To Change or Not To Change

Your Choice Will Make You Bitter or Better

by Dr. M. Duane Rawlins

Amuzement Publications

Acknowledgment

I am so grateful to the many friends who have taught me many of the concepts I have shared in this book. My wife Lee Ann and our close friend Barbara Overgaard have helped me a great deal with typing and editing. My son Matthew has also assisted me in publishing the book.

I want to dedicate this book to each of my fifteen grandchildren who I hope will read and enjoy learning from their grandfather who loves them very much.

Preface

"Therefore if any man be in Christ, he is a new creature: old things are passed away: All things are become new." 2 Corinthians 5:17

Life is made up of many seasons of change. Change is one of the most consistent things that happen in our lives. Much of the time we are not fully prepared for the changes that take place as we move through life. This book is an accumulation of over 70 years of experiences, which has included numerous changes. I changed vocations from education to business at age 45. My entire family moved from California to Oregon at the same time. When I was 57 my first wife died. At age 62, I lost my 37 year-old son to cancer. These are only a few of the major changes that have taken place in my life. We can learn from others and our life experiences, or we can learn from "the school of hard knocks" It is our choice.

Change does not belong to one age group. Life at every stage is full of changes, and it's how we respond to change that determines whether we move forward or get stuck in the past. Changes in schools and homes, changes in marriages, life and death, friendships are among the variety of arenas in which humans experience change.

As we grow older, many of us resist change and challenges because we have settled into a comfort zone based on life-long habits and experiences. It's true that in our senior years we are intellectually superior to the days of our youth, but security and familiarity bring us comfort and satisfaction. Complacency sets in, and we no longer discover the wonderful opportunities to explore life and enjoy changes that will enrich our lives. But, even the oldest person reading this book has the opportunity to decide how they will respond to change.

Life is all about relationship, loving people, enjoying each day to the fullest. I have enjoyed writing this book, and sharing the wisdom of a life filled with rich experiences that have brought about significant changes in my life. I hope you will enjoy sharing these experiences, and learning from them as well.

Introduction

How has change affected your life?

What has brought about
the greatest amount of change in your life
in recent months?
It may be a serious health problem
such as a heart attack or cancer.
Maybe you changed jobs or retired.
Perhaps it was a move to another city.
Maybe you're adjusting to a body
that doesn't function like it used to.
Or maybe it is a new marriage.
For me change came when I watched
the men from the funeral home
carry my wife out of our bedroom
in a black bag.

For LeeAnn, my present wife,
change meant one minute having
a healthy husband by her side,
and the next having him
die in her arms
of an aneurysm in his chest.
Change affects us in so many ways,
and I want to help you cope with it.

It does get better

It had been almost a year since Betty died,
and I was beginning to realize that my life
really was changing,
mostly in a positive way.
The pain was not quite so deep.
I had begun to learn how important it is
to live in true humility.
My teaching was more effective.
I was far more sensitive to others' hurts and
wounds.
Deep healing had taken place.
I was learning how to treat my life partner
should I have a chance to marry again.
I was starting to feel alive again and more whole.
All God needed was a willing heart.
I began to realize there were new mountains to
move,

new relationships to develop,
new books to write,
and maybe even a new partner
to enjoy life with.
I prayed and sought God for the qualities that I would want
in a new mate.
He gave me my heart's desire
by introducing me to LeeAnn Smucker
who had lost her husband
a little over two years earlier.
We spent time together and began to realize
that we had much in common
and much to celebrate.

Lonliness provokes change

When I got alone, usually at night,
I still found myself very lonely
and I felt incomplete.
After teaching in Singapore at the
Youth With A Mission base,
I decided to start celebrating change.
I would like to share what I have learned about celebrating change.
It has been my practice
to spend time alone with God and His word
on a daily basis.
This habit was the greatest help and support
as I began to celebrate change.
Isaiah 61:1-3 began to take on new meaning:
"The Spirit of the Lord God is upon Me,
because the Lord has anointed me

to preach good tidings to the poor:
He has sent Me to heal the brokenhearted
to proclaim liberty to the captives,
and the opening of the prison
to those who are bound,
to proclaim the acceptable year of the Lord,
and the day of vengeance of our God;
to comfort all who mourn,
to console those who mourn in Zion,
to give them beauty for ashes,
the oil of joy for mourning,
the garment of praise
for the spirit of heaviness." (NKJV)

We all have unanswered questions

Change requires us to move out of our comfort
zone.
When we do that,
there are many natural road blocks
that cause us to want to back up and stay
where we are.
Questions and fears began to rise in my mind
in the midst of change.
Fear of the unknown,
fear of new and unfamiliar surroundings,
uncertainty about what to say or do, and
questions like:
Was it really possible that God still had a rich, full
life for me to live?
Out of these ashes could I receive wonderful
new blessings?

Would I experience joy and happiness in my
senior years?
How long am I going to feel like this?
What must I do to accept that which has taken
place?
Who can help me walk through this?
Will I ever be better?
Is it okay to fear that which is unknown?
Could I really find joy in the midst of suffering?
As you continue to read,
I trust that you will find answers
to these profound
and very real questions.

Change is not easy

"You must never be fearful about what you are doing when it is right." Rosa Parks

Fear of the unknown
is natural.
When we make a change
fear is often present
because we have not done it this way
before.
There are all kinds of forces attempting
to keep us from changing.
One is our enemy, the devil.
He wants to keep us looking back,
yearning for yesterday.
It's difficult to move into a new relationship
when it's unclear what tomorrow will
bring.

Often God will ask us to let go of something
without revealing what's on the other side.

Planning for the future reduces fear and uncertainty.

Plan for the future
but don't try to live in it.

Desire and hope

Desire is one of the first steps towards healthy change.

God has promised to give us the desires of our heart.
We must cooperate by allowing
new seeds of desire to be planted.
Hope is also necessary.
This means we have a confident expectation
of something good in our future.
Next comes faith, "the substance of things hoped for,
the evidence of things unseen" (Heb. 11:1).
Peace should begin to settle in
as you experience positive change.
Peace is the chief ally of effective change.
Knowing this, I decided to celebrate change.
Why is it so important to celebrate change?

Why can't we just endure it, accept, and adapt
without celebrating it?
"Every good thing comes from God" (James 1:17).
We need not only to acknowledge the change
but also learn to appreciate it.
David said he would
"Bless the Lord at all times" (Ps. 34:1).
Romans 8:28 reminds us that all things
work together for our good.
We are also reminded by Paul to rejoice
in the Lord always (Phil.4:4).
These words make it very clear that we are to celebrate,
not tolerate,
change.

Getting back on track

When we move out of marriage
by death or divorce,
we move into a new season.
Whether we like it or not
our lives must change.
We can fight it or accept it.
It takes much time and
lots of prayer to get back on track.
We are shoved out of our
comfort zone, and we don't like it at all.
Drink liberally from grace,
Pray daily for mercy,
Pour yourself into something
you enjoy.
Let time pass by.
Declare where you are.
Don't hide from it.
Tell the truth about where
you are.
Stop pretending it doesn't hurt.
Tell God about it.

Look for new ways to find
joy and meaningful activity.
Look for and enjoy the beauty
around you.

Swallow change
or it will slallow you

One facet of change that is difficult to deal with
is that many times in the initial stages,
change looks bad;
it feels bad from every side,
and it's hard to swallow.
Here is where we need to take a deep breath
and accept the change.
You cannot remember and forget at the same time,
just as you cannot forgive and indict
at the same time.
With my mind I need to forget.
With my heart I need to forgive.
Both involve a choice.
My mind and heart have to be in agreement.
God has an unconditional guarantee that

"He will make everything work for good
to those who love God and are called
according to His purpose" (Romans 8:28).
He gives grace to the humble.
His grace is sufficient.
You must choose what you will do
when it comes to making changes
you don't like.
Change now, receive the grace,
and exalt as you move forward.

Keep on changing

"For things to change we must change. For things to get better we must get better." Heidi Wills

Be very careful about getting stuck in a rut.

Life is full of changes.

Some people believe that they can do the same thing over and over again, and get different results.

This is called insanity.

Learn from your past and do things differently.

You cannot change the past but you can learn from it.

There will be challenges to face and changes to make.

Keep yourself moving in the right direction.

Most likely it will not be easy. It certainly will be better

when you know who you are,
where you are,
and where you are going.
Life is a journey through time,
filled with many choices.
Dream your own dreams and realize
it's up to you to succeed.
Nobody will do it for you.
Stay focused on things that have eternal value.

It is never too late to change

"What you do right now will have an accumulated effect on all our tomorrows."
Alexandra Studdland

The important thing to remember is that
you can change the path you are on
at any given time.
Sometimes we come to a place
where we have to make a decision
about which road to travel.
You might think of it as a crossroads.
I recommend the road less traveled,
the one that fits your style, gifts,
interests and purpose.
You are the only one who can fulfill your dreams.
It's good to get counsel, but the final decision is yours.

Take control and determine your destiny.
Operate within the set of standards or principles
you have selected as appropriate to you.
God seems to be the fastest checker player in the world
because it's always your move.
He has done all that is necessary.
Now it's up to you.

True humility in change

Are you a knight in shining armor
    or a skunk in a tin can?
Intimacy with God will do away with your need
    to put up a phony front.
Look deeply within, acknowledge who you really
    are.
Stop looking for protection.
Come boldly before your heavenly Father
    and tell it like it is.
Tell the truth about yourself.
Smile. Your face won't crack.
Let down your defenses and you will find
    that people are much more
        comfortable around you.
It's what's on the inside of your heart that counts.
True humility is being known for who you are.

As you change the way you think
people will like you
because of your realness and
openness.

Getting started right

"Be sure you put your feet in the right place, then stand firm." Abraham Lincoln

At the beginning of each new day
thank God you're still alive
and able to change.

Be careful not to waste time fretting about yesterday.
We certainly want to learn from our mistakes
        but that does not mean we dwell on them.
Live in the now, enjoy each moment.
Don't try to change everything
        but select those items you see
        as most important
        and do them.

Be careful to plan for the future
but don't go there too often.
"Sufficient for the day is its own trouble"
(Matt. 6:34).
Live one day at a time
and live it to the fullest.

Change the way you eat

"Act as if what you do makes a difference."
William James

As I look around I see a significant number of
people
Who are overweight
or sickly in their appearance.
Someone has said that you are what you eat.
I watched a video recently
where a man conducted a
one-month experiment.
By eating all of his meals from a fast-food
restaurant,
he gained twenty-five pounds.
He developed serious health problems.
We are all very different,
with different frames.

Our bodies require different amounts of food.
There are hundreds of diets being touted today.
I am not recommending that you diet.
But I am saying that most of us need
to eat healthier food
and less of it.

Discontentment and lack of gratefulness

Discontentment keeps us outside
His courts of praise and thanksgiving.
It results in bitterness, and opens the door
for so many other negative attitudes to creep in.
Anger, greed, jealousy and many other forms of evil
will make their way into our hearts.
Rest and discontentment have nothing in common.
Another strong enemy of change is complacency.
It gives the false impression of being
content and confident.
It may even portray faith but down deep it is full of
apathy,
pride,
and fear.

It is the act of avoiding change.
Some level of fear is normal when we
move into the unknown
so the real question is,
how do we handle it ?
It is absolutely imperative that we embrace
change
if we are going to reach our destiny.

Change the way you think regarding finance

"Keep your lives free from the love of money and be content with what you have" (Hebrews 13:5).

The world around us uses all types of advertising
to produce discontentment.
Paul the apostle stated it this way:
"I have learned to be content in
whatever state I am in" (Phil. 4:11).
As I look around I see a constant desire for more
We need to ask ourselves the hard question,
"How much is enough?"
It seems that the most common answer is
"a little bit more."
We are a product of all our previous experiences
and thoughts regarding money.
If we are to change the way we think and act
in regards to finances, it must be
planned and purposeful.

If you abuse the use of credit cards
    it will not be easy to change that habit.
It will take willpower and a clear strategy
    to get out of debt.
It can be done, but it will definitely
    require a change in your conduct.
One powerful way to improve
    is to stop impulse purchases.
Take more time before you make
    emotional decisions.

Life is an adventure

"The future belongs to those who believe in the beauty of their dreams. In the long run we really do shape our own lives; and then together we shape the world around us. The process never ends until we die."

Eleanor Roosevelt

We are never too old to learn.
I am happy to say I am 76 years young
    and learning something new every week.
I am willing to make changes.
In fact, I often wonder
    what I am going to be when I grow up.
My life has been, and still is,
    full of exciting adventures.
We just returned from two weeks in India,
    and I am a changed man.
I have a greater desire to aid and assist
    children at risk
        than ever before.
I encourage you to see life as an adventure.
Explore the world around you.

Be aware of the beauty that surrounds you every
day.
Learn to experience every unique situation
and learn from it.
Search for the true meaning of life
and bring joy to each person
that you contact on life's pathway.

The dot

At our moment of conception on planet earth
a great deal about who we are is
determined.
Our frame,
our height,
the color of our eyes, etc.
Our time on earth will determine what we will be
forever and ever.
Everything we do, say, and think has great value
because together with God, we are
determining what we will be throughout eternity.
Our life on earth could be represented by a dot
compared to the very long line of eternity.
We are on a journey.
We are being prepared to rule and
reign with Christ forever.

You and God are determining your destiny.
You are constantly growing and
changing in some direction.
You get to have a large hand in your future
by making right choices.
So live your dream, discover your purpose
and enjoy life.

Embracing change

"I am only one but I am one. I cannot do everything but I still can do something. And because I cannot do everything, I will not refuse to do the something I can do." Helen Keller.

Change affects our day, every day.
It cannot be avoided.
I trust that after reading this book
and seeing the many facets of change
you will be quicker to accept it,
ready to acknowledge it,
and see it as an opportunity to grow.
Learn to be less intimidated by it.
See it as a friend.
Smile when you see it happening.
Make the best of it.
And when trouble comes,
remember it came to pass,
it didn't come to stay.
See it as a chance to be yourself
as your stumble through life.

Think and grow rich

"Enrich the lives of thousands, one person at a time."

Duane Rawlins

Years ago I read a book by the above title,
and it greatly impacted my life.
In many ways we are the sum product of what we think.
In the Bible Jesus says,
"For as a man thinks in his heart, so is he" (Prov. 23:7).
My first impression of this verse was that it was about
growing financially rich
but that is only part of the equation.
We need to be rich in every aspect of our lives.
Our thinking (what we dwell on) has
a profound influence

on how we live.
So many times our health is impacted by our thoughts.
We worry about yesterday and tomorrow
instead of enjoying the moment in which we live.
God's word says, "Fix your thoughts
on what is true and honorable and right.
Think about things that are pure, lovely, and admirable," (Phil. 4:8, Living Bible).

Where is your focus?

"But don't begin until you count the cost for who would begin construction of a building without first getting estimates and then checking to see if there is enough money to pay the bills," (Luke 14:28 Living Bible).

A lack of planning,
both in our work and in our lives
is the common reason we fall short
of our dreams and our goals.
Planning takes much of the guesswork
out of what we do each day.
We are more likely to spend time
on things that don't matter and
leave less time for things that
really need our attention,
when we don't plan our work and
work our plan.
The key is to live a focused life
if we want to accomplish our dreams.
The more we learn from the past and let go of it,
the more we can focus on the present.
Positive change will then begin to take place.

What difference will you make?

Life moves forward day by day.
Each of us has a chance
    to make a difference.
Mother Teresa made a real difference
    in the lives of lonely dying people.
Each one of us has different gifts or talents.
Therefore our expression will be
    very different from everyone else's.
Ask yourself, "What difference will this make
    one hundred years from today?"
Each of us creates the roads we will follow.
There are millions of options to analyze
    as we move through life.
Every deed has value.
It is very rewarding when we complete a task
    that has eternal value.

You can make a real difference in peoples' lives
by doing random acts of kindness.
Everyone needs to feel love and appreciated

Live your life by principles

"Cease to live by rules and regulations. The letter of the law kills," (2 Cor. 3:6).

Rules and regulations tend
to move us towards legalism.
If you are going to change
into the person you want to be,
it's important to develop a set of principles
that you wish to live by.

Notice we are talking about principles.
They need to be carefully selected
to assist you in living out the concepts
that are most meaningful to you.
Jesus' Sermon on the Mount
is a wonderful resource
to help you develop your own guidelines.

Words that express some of our principles are
love, joy, peace, patience, kindness,
honesty,
purity, wholeness and self control

Lighten up, nobody's perfect

Every prayer that we pray
    is a prayer for change.
We have all sinned and fallen short
    of the glory of God.
Abraham lied and said his wife was his sister.
David committed adultery with Bathsheba.
Jacob deceived his father
    in order to obtain his older brother's
    blessing.
Peter swore and denied that he knew Jesus.

So lighten up. We all miss the mark.
It's not how many times you fall that counts
    but it's how many times you repent, get up,
    and keep on doing your best.
Learn from your mistakes.
Give yourself the privilege of being human.

Enjoy the moment.
Believe that God has forgiven you.
Then forgive yourself

It's all about Jesus

If we want to become
all that we were designed to be,
then we need to realize that
it's all about Him,
not about us.
He is the only one who lived the perfect life.
He needs to be our model, our Savior, and our King.
As we grow in intimacy with God the Father,
God the Son,
and God the Holy Spirit,
we will become like them.
Change will take place and
we will be transformed into His likeness.
Jesus reminded his disciples,
"If you have seen me you have seen the Father."

He also said, "I do nothing except
that which the Father tells me to do" (John 14:9).
To do and be as Jesus---this should be
our heart's desire.
As it becomes a part of our way of life,
we will be changed from glory to glory.

Are you true to yourself?

Many times people operate in the belief
that if they don't deal with, think about or
talk about their fears and beliefs,
they don't exist.
We need to learn to be congruent
so that our insides and our outsides
(words and actions) match.
Often our body language sends
a completely different message than our
words.
Some people are constantly holding up a false face
for fear people will see
the real person behind the face.
It's time to start accepting who you are.
Refuse to compare yourself with any other person.
Know that you are the only one of your kind.
Comparison is always harmful.

Its fruit is poison.
Enjoy yourself whether you are a one-talent person
    or a five-talent person.
A little boy said,
    "I ain't much but I'm all I got."
Isn't it time to be who you are
    and enjoy liking yourself?

It's up to you

"Work out your own salvation, for God is at work within you both to do and to will according to His good pleasure" (Phil. 2:12).

No one will live your life for you.
Others may listen or give you sound advice
but the truth is you are the one
who must make the final decision.
You must know yourself and your gifts
well enough to know what is right for you.
It is so helpful to focus on your strengths.
Too often we give most of our time and energy
trying to improve our weaknesses.
Learn to operate in your strengths and
spend less time focusing on your
weaknesses.

They will soon fall away.
Life is far too short to worry about the things
that you cannot do well.
It's also a waste of time to expect someone else
to accomplish your dreams for you.

Allow the Holy Spirit to guide you

"Do not be drunk with wine but be drunk with the Spirit," (Eph.5:18).

Excessive drinking will get you into big trouble.
The above scripture encourages us
to be mastered,
gripped,
and controlled by the Holy Spirit.
When we are drunk we are out of control.
We often do foolish things.
But when we are led by the Spirit
we do all kinds of godly stuff.
The intimacy that comes from practicing His presence
will change your life.
We need to listen to that still small voice.

Perhaps it's too noisy at your house to hear
anything
but the roar of the crowd.
Get alone with God with the specific purpose
of hearing His voice.
Then obey His counsel.
As you align yourself with His will
you will sense a wonderful change taking
place.

Dare to disclose

The time has come for you to be honest with yourself.
Starting today, why not declare who you really are?
Stop hiding from yourself and others.
You are not the first person to feel
insecure and inadequate.
Disclose those things that are holding you back.
Share your heart with someone more mature than you.
God's word says, "Confess your faults to one another" (James 5:16).
Someone once said that we must reveal
our wounds and hurts
before God will heal them.
When we operate in humility
we are merely attempting to be known
for who we are.

We can relax and quit wasting so much energy
trying to prove to others
that we are someone
that we really are not.

Get over it

There is a song by this title that really speaks to
me.
It points out many things that go wrong in our
lives,
then suggests a very simple answer---
"Get over it."
Most of us hold on to and cherish our excuses.
We don't want to let them go
because we use them to complain and
rationalize why we can't accomplish a task or
reach a goal.
If we are to truly change and
become the person we want to be, then we
have to learn to "get over it."

We can live in yesterday's failures and
whine about how cruel life is, or
we can learn from life,

get over it,
and seek to fulfill our dream.
Do you really want to be like Him? Develop
patience and grow?
Then realize the best way to accomplish this
is to respond correctly to the thoughtless,
insensitive people who invade your life.
You will be ridiculed and criticized
if you take a strong righteous stand.
What is your dream?

"I can do all things through Christ who
strengthens me" (Phil. 4:13).
It's hard to live your dream
if you don't know what it is.
At the end of the day or week
it's hard to know how well you did
unless you know what you were supposed
to do.
You must decide which path you want to take and
what goal you want to accomplish.
All of us have the capacity to dream.
In most cases we will never accomplish our dream
without taking risks.

Give your mind the freedom
        to move outside the box.
Dreams have a way of seeming impossible.
That might be a good way of determining
        whether it is a good dream.
Your dream will most likely be different
        from anyone else's
                because you are unique,
                        the only one of your kind.
Catch this concept,
        and you can make one giant leap forward.

Learn to live your dream

Remember that most likely your dream will be
    what you do best and enjoy the most.
Fear of the unknown will begin to surface.
The enemy will try to convince you
    that you are nobody with nothing to give.
Often it's difficult to verbalize your dream.
When you receive a big dream,
    it will seem overwhelming at first.

As you search out your dream,
    remember what you loved to do as a youth.
As you work on your dream ask yourself,
"What would I most want to be remembered for?"
As your dream takes shape you will begin to
realize, "This is what I was created for."
Living on the edge will always generate
    fear and uncertainty.

As you leave your comfort zone, remember that
nobody really enjoys doing that.
Use your courage to move through and beyond
the fear.
Remove the fear of people and
the fear of failure from your life.
Remember it's time to be great before it's too late.
Learn to live large for God.

Define your dream

"Efforts and courage are not enough without purpose and direction." John F. Kennedy

It is most important that you have a dream.
First things first.
Identify your dream, and be sure it is clear.
It should be big enough
that you cannot accomplish it on your own.
It will require you to change and take chances.
Be someone who inspires the people around you
by the way you live out your dream.
Take advantage of the opportunity when it happens.
Don't worry about tomorrow.
Today's troubles are enough.
Look forward to problems and challenges

and fully accept both the struggles
and the joys that come with your
dreams.
God is the ultimate dreamgiver,
but we must have open minds and hearts,
and
be ready to move forward
to accomplish our dreams.
If you are unwilling to make changes you greatly
reduce the chances
of accomplishing your dream.

Teamwork makes dreams work
"Coming together is a beginning. Keeping together is a process. Working together is success." John Maxwell
A team can help you to accomplish
more than you can do by yourself.
It frees you to do what you do best.
It will make it possible for you to work
in your strengths and work
around your weaknesses.
Teamwork can help you fulfill the desires of your
heart.

No problem is insurmountable.
With courage and determination
you and your team can overcome anything.

Andrew Carnegie once said,
"It marks a big step in your development when you come to realize that other people can help you do a better job than you can do alone."
Learn to spend time with people different from you
so that you can learn to grow and change.
Enjoy differences rather than fighting them.
Remember the slogan:
Together
Everyone
Accomplishes
More

Keeping the dream alive

"We must learn to live together as brothers or perish together as fools."

Martin Luther King, Jr.

First you must dare to dream. Then,
prepare your dream,
wear your dream, and
share your dream.
Keep your goals out of reach
but not out of sight.
Walt Disney said: "If you can dream it, you can do it.
Never lose sight of the fact that
this whole thing was started by a mouse."
Make no small plans for they have
no power to stir men's souls.

"The successful attainment of a dream is a
cart-and-horse affair.
Without a team of horses,
a cart full of dreams can go nowhere."
Ray Murphy

Be a doer as well as a dreamer

"He who looks into the perfect law of liberty and continues in it, and is not a forgetful hearer but a doer of the word, this one will be blessed in what he does" (James 1:25).

James goes on to say in chapter three, verse 13, "Who is wise and understanding among you? Let him show by good conduct that his works are done

in the meekness of wisdom."

Clearly we must not be daydreamers.

We need to put feet to our dreams through wise actions.

Another way of saying it is,

"An ounce of prevention is worth a pound of cure."

We need to plan carefully and think before we act,
	but we must act or do.
Some people are so fascinated by work
	that they can sit and watch by the hour.
Let people catch your vision or dream by what you do,
	not just by what you say.
We need to keep doing, trying new things
	because that's what life is all about.

Not every dream comes true

It is unrealistic to assume
that every dream must come true.
Often as we develop our dream,
new facts or circumstances will arise
which make it necessary to alter the dream,
or move on to a new dream.
Part of the joy of life
is found in the pursuit of a dream.
Often we find out
that our dream doesn't work or
that a certain door will not open.
At those times we tend to feel like a failure
or want to condemn ourselves and others.
We need to realize
we are never a failure
unless we quit completely.
So it's time to move on
to a new dream or vision.

Each experience is a part of life.
No one accomplishes all that he sets out to do.
The completeness of our lives
    does not depend on
    all our dreams being perfected.
For as long as we live
    we will encounter challenges
    that require us to change.

Competition

"We have not come to compete with one another. We have come to complete one another.." Bill McCartney

Competition has been central in my life.
Ever since I can remember I have been competitive.
It seemed to be in my genes.
As a young man my motto was
"Show me a good loser
and I'll show you a loser."
The attitude reflected in that statement has
changed significantly in my senior years.
One of my favorite stories is about Winston Churchhill.
As Prime Minister of England, speaking to the students

of the school where he attended as a youth,
he said,
"Never, never, never, never, never give up."
Those words were his total speech.
That character quality of persistence has greatly motivated me
in my desire to be the best I can be.
I trust you are the kind of person who does his best to be the best he can be.
If we avoid comparing ourselves with others
and know that we are unique,
then we can feel very good about who we are.

Change the way you think

"So act that your principle of action might safely be made law for the whole world."

Immanuel Kant.

It has become very clear that it is our attitude about life
that really matters.
It is not our problems in life that make the difference
but how we respond to them.
Ninety percent of everything is attitude.
As we learn to change the way we think,
life will become more pleasant.
There truly is power in thinking positively.
Count your blessings rather than your problems.
No one can upset you unless you choose to be upset.

As long as our heart is right
and we keep a positive long-range view,
the bumps in the road are much less
unsettling.

It's okay to be lonely for a little while

It's okay to be lonely
and not have to pretend
that everything is fine,
that you're always on time,
that poems all must rhyme.

It's okay to be lonely,
and you don't have to hide your tears
or carry a smile around for years
or deny or cover up your fears.

It's okay to be lonely
to say you've had a bad day
that you just want to get away
and maybe, just maybe
you want to be lonely…for a little while.[1]

You are unique

As you read through this book
you will notice certain themes
that seem to be repeated several times.
This is done on purpose.
I believe that most of us do not comprehend
or make a concept part of our life
the first time we read it.
Often it takes three or four times
before we really catch it.
Therefore, I am reminding you
how unique each one of us is.
We are indeed special,
one of a kind.
Realize that God not only loves you
but He likes you.
Learn to accept your uniqueness
And never compare yourself
to anyone else.

Just look at your finger prints.
Out of billions of people you have your own set
    and you can be distinguished from all
    others
Because of the uniqueness of your fingerprints.
Take joy in this amazing reality
    and enjoy the journey with God.

What truly brings you joy?

"Study to show yourself approved unto God as a workman that needs not to be ashamed, handling aright the Word of God" (2 Tim. 2:15).

Over the years
I have discovered what brings me great joy:
reading God's Word and listening to others,
rather than learning from the school of
hard knocks.
What brings you joy?
I personally find great joy
in being a vessel of love.
I also greatly enjoy reading, learning, and
growing.
That brings me joy.
Get to know yourself, your feelings, your gifts,
your priorities, your successes.

God said the fruit of the Spirit is
Love, joy, peace, patience
Kindness, goodness, faithfulness
And self-control (Gal. 5:22).
Often the joy is removed from our lives
by allowing problems to grow
until they become large dilemmas.
Fear is normal, especially when we move into the unknown.
It is okay to walk slowly in the dark,
and to be careful
when we are unsure of our footing.
But do not let fear overtake you
and crowd out the joy.
Joy belongs to you.

Cultivate an attitude of gratitude

According to Charles Swindoll,
90% of everything is attitude.
Therefore if gratitude is one of our foundational principles,
and we fill our thoughts with gratitude,
we will go through each change in life
with a spirit of gratefulness.
If we are careful to identify our hopes and dreams
as well as our foundational principles,
when we need them they will be there.
In all of life, with its constant changes,
perception is one of the keys to happiness.
It is how we perceive life and its many challenges
that really makes the difference.
The soldiers of Israel saw Goliath as too big to hit,
but David saw him as too big to miss.

We need to know who we are
        and the abilities we possess.
This self-knowledge will equip us to face life's changes
        and feel good about our accomplishments.

Is your "child" still alive?

Each of us has a child hidden away in our heart.
He or she will occasionally surface, and
        needs to be given permission
        to enjoy the moment.
Our adult nature may tend to consider the child heart
        as silly and inappropriate.
But we need to allow our childlike nature
        to enjoy a few moments of sheer fun.
Perhaps laughing with others over nothing,
        until our sides hurt.
There is a time for the adult in us to take over
        and be responsible,
        a time to put away the toys
        and take up the tools.
However, there is a time to let go,

feel free from all of life's burdens
and enjoy the moment.
Many of us take life too seriously.
We need to laugh at ourselves
and realize that much of what seems
overwhelming
Will soon pass.
I love the phrase,
"It came to pass, it didn't come to stay."
Isn't it time to enjoy life
and love the little one
that lives inside of us?

God's Word will change your life

It's been said that one must tune his violin
before he plays in the orchestra.
Therefore we should tune our hearts
by spending our early hours
alone
with God
Meditating on His word.

I have traveled a great deal,
teaching in over 30 countries.
Things look very different.
from 5,000 feet in the air
The sky is always clear
and the stars are bright.
The same seems to be true
when we get God's perspective.

Early in the morning
learn to start your day off right.
If you want to obey God
then start by being in His Word
until you get revelation
which will give you motivation
which will make obeying easier.
The key here is to align ourselves
with His will
which will cause us
to feel whole and complete.

Simplify your life

Learn to put first things first.
The world around us will
Try to force us into its
    "hurry up" mode.
We are constantly barraged with advertisements
    that push us to buy a bigger car,
    house, boat, or more clothes.
We need to answer the hard question,
    "How much is enough?"
Most of us need to take another look at our priorities,
    slow down,
        and smell the roses.
We fool ourselves into thinking
    that life is more complicated than it really is.

We become confused by what appears to be
wants that are presented as needs.
When we look a bit harder,
things are not so confusing.
Words like, "Love one another,"
"Believe in each person's worth or value,"
"Conduct random acts of kindness,"
"Listen more and talk less,"
"Live simpler and enjoy life,"
take on a much deeper meaning.

Nature has much to teach us

"One day is as a thousand years and a thousand years is as a day with God" (2 Peter 3:8).

Does it amaze you when you observe how fish,
    especially salmon,
    return to the same stream where they spawned?
Or the teamwork towards a common goal
    in a hill of ants
    or a hive of bees?
God placed in animals, fish and insects
    all kinds of instincts that we cannot help but marvel at.

Learn to live out your destiny.
Be what you were designed to be.
Goats and deer have hinds feet

so they never stumble moving swiftly
over the mountain.
But horses must watch where they go
less they stumble and fall
Creatures do not alter their existence
to be like others.
Nor should we.
Nature is not intimidated
by anyone.
Nor should we be.

What is your complaint?

I complained about not having shoes
until I met a man
who had no feet.
I complained about wearing glasses
until I met a man
who was blind.
I complained about being underpaid on the job
until I met a man
who had no job.
You can look around you
and find all kinds of people
who have far greater problems than yours.
It's time to take our eyes off our problems
and start counting our blessings.
If we do this, we will begin
to be much more tolerant,
and caring of others.

When we focus on others faults,
our world begins to suddenly look bad.
Regroup,
look for the good in others,
encourage those around you.

His last words

Please read this page carefully.
They are the last words of a young man
who was unable to follow his own advice.
Learn from his mistake.

"We truly do remain true
to our methods of escaping.
We don't want to see the real world
or our real lives.
We want a candy-coated reality,
someone else's superior existence.
Life is what you make it.
You decide your own destiny.
Choose wisely;
break away from the quiet desperation,
from the mass of men who are miserable
You must be your own person.

Think for yourself, and
    don’t let other people think for you.
Achieve your goals;
    don’t do what someone else wants you to
    do.
Forget escaping life;
    enjoy it.
The more you really want to,
    the more you truly will.”
His life ended abruptly.
What will you do with yours?

Most of us love to be in control

We want to determine our own fate.
We need to retain the final decision.
We want the power to make things
        go the way we want them to go.
If only we could get enough of it
        everything would be all right.
We all have the illusion that
        if I am in control
        if I can just get the right amount of power
I can control the world, and it will be
        a safe place to live.
The challenge is
Letting go of control,
        trusting in the Lord,
        recognizing Him as the final authority.
It is not easy when we let go and let God.

We will find the joy and peace
we are looking for.
Seek Him first,
let Him add to your life
that which He imparts to you.
Situations no longer become so important.
One can celebrate change
knowing the God
who never changes
is in control.

Take a good look in the mirror

Each day as I look in the mirror
    I see changes taking place.
My hair is thinner,
    there are wrinkles around my eyes and
    my forehead is much larger than it used to
    be.
No question about it,
    I am aging.
I trip over the rug
    trying to jump off a three foot wall.
Seems life threatening.

At my age (76), 10-year plans don't make much
sense.
But I do feel like I have much left
    that I want to do
    and very little time to make it happen.

I don't want to waste time on unimportant issues.
I still have time to get my life going.
Change is what encourages us
to be more of what God has planned for us.
1 Cor. 2:9 puts it this way,
"No eye has seen
Nor ear has heard
And no mind has imagined
What God has prepared for those
Who love Him."

It is later than we think,
So let's do our best
and make the best of who we are.

Free from bondage

Many of us are shackled
by earlier mistakes
that we haven't taken care of.
We have pushed them down
into our subconscious where we think
we do not have to deal with them.
When they surface
we push them back down again.
They often return to haunt us at most
inopportune times.
Bondage sets in after several years
of this type of action.
Is this bondage in your life?
Has bitterness set in to such an extent that when
certain problems arise, you explode?
It's time to be set free.

Seek help,
        admit your have a problem.
Purpose in your heart
        to allow God to set you completely free.
Give up your desire for revenge.
Break down,
        pray,
        and ask God to help you forgive.

Right choices in life

Life is all about making good choices.
As we travel through life
        and clarify what we want out of life,
        with careful planning
        we can be prepared to make
                that choice when there is a fork
                in the road.
When a crisis sets in,
        we need to not only make the right choice
        but also to follow it up
        with a disciplined life that lives it out
        on a daily basis.
We can and will make a difference
        when we enthusiastically meet life
                head on
                with a positive mental attitude.

Follow through on your ideas
and your dreams.
Learn to finish a project or dream
before starting a new one.
See the good that is all around.
Learn to accentuate the positive
and eliminate the negative.
Smile, God loves you.
You have much more to offer
than you think.

Do you have self-esteem issues?

Here are some questions to dwell on:
Do you sometimes catch yourself exaggerating
about the importance of your job or role?
Do you compare your behavior
to the standards of others?
Are you jealous of the positions, possessions
or opportunities of others?
Is it hard for you to admit that you make mis
takes?
Do you put people down
so you can feel good about yourself?
Are you a bully, demanding your own way?
Do you feel insecure and inadequate
when faced with change?
Is it hard to accept compliments and
say a simple thank you?

These are some indications that you may have
some self-esteem issues
that need your attention.

Everyone has the same amount of time

Many of us feel
that there just is not enough time
to accomplish what we want.
The truth is, everyone has exactly
the same amount of time.
You cannot turn back the hands of time
but you can use your time more profitably
to do what you deem important.
Some of us tend to procrastinate
putting off until tomorrow
what should be done now.
You are the only one
who can decide to
"Just do it."
The truth is, when you take chances
and do the important things,
progress begins to take place.

When you are filled with enthusiasm
and act upon your dreams
miracles seem to take place.

Stop pretending you're someone you're not

God identified himself
when Moses asked,
"Who shall I say sent me?"
by telling him,
"I Am" sent you.
There was a television show years ago
in which they tried to get you to guess
who was the real person among three
guests.
They would ask,
Will the real Bob Jones please stand?"
We need to be more willing
to have our true identity revealed,
and stop pretending
we are someone that we are not.
Let the real you shine through.

Be comfortable with who you are.
Let God's love shine through your life
so that people can see the beautiful
person that you are.
Make your passage through life
be an endless journey of love.

Sing your own song

This may seem like an odd title
    because few of us are song writers.
I can hardly carry a tune.
However, there is a special meaning here.
First of all, Christianity
    is the only religion that has singing
    as an integral part
    of its message.
We sing because we're happy.
Each of us has much to sing about
    and there is something about singing
    that lifts our spirits.
I recently attended a funeral service for
    a young 19-year-old boy
    who died in a car accident.
There were wonderful songs

that had been written for the occasion
of remembering him.
The entire evening was filled
with celebration
because of the great faith,
hope, and love of this family.
I plan to sing my own song
that represents who I am and
the strong faith in God who created me.

Learn to be a lover

If I could speak in any language in heaven or on earth but didn't love others,

I would only be making meaningless noise like a loud gong or a clanging cymbal.

If I had the gift of prophecy, and if I knew all the mysteries of the future and knew everything about everything, but didn't love others, what good would I be?

And if I had the gift of faith so that I could speak to a mountain and make it move, without love I would be no good to anybody.

If I gave everything I have to the poor and even sacrificed my body, I could boast about it; but if I didn't love others, I would be of no value whatsoever.

Love is patient and kind. Love is not jealous or boastful or proud or rude.

Love does not demand its own way.
Love is not irritable, and it keeps no record of when it has been wronged.
It is never glad about injustice but rejoices whenever the truth wins out.
Love never gives up, never loses faith, is always hopeful, and endures through every circumstance.
Love will last forever, but prophecy and speaking in unknown languages
and special knowledge will all disappear.

Now we know only a little, and even the gift of prophecy reveals little!
But when the end comes, these special gifts will all disappear.
It's like this: When I was a child, I spoke and thought and reasoned as a child does.
But when I grew up, I put away childish things.
Now we see things imperfectly as in a poor mirror,
but then we will see everything with perfect clarity.
All that I know now is partial and incomplete, but then I will know everything completely,

just as God knows me now.
There are three things that will endure
— faith, hope, and love —
and the greatest of these is love.

I Corinthians 13 Forgive and forget (New Living Translation)

When Peter asked Jesus
"How many times must we forgive…
seven times?"
Jesus responded,
"No, seventy times seven."
In other words, there is no limit.
We must keep on forgiving.
This does not mean we must trust
the offender.
Trust is built on proven behavior.
The forgiveness is for our own benefit
as much as it is for the one
who committed the offense.
Forgiveness restores our energy to go on
Often we must ask God to give us the grace
to forgive.

If we are indeed going to change and move on
    and not get stuck in a rut
    we must learn to forgive.
If we relax,
    begin to appreciate the gifts of others,
    and have a more forgiving spirit,
    we would be on our way to inner healing
    and a changed life.

Before you leave

It has always been my desire
to leave a legacy.
I want my children to have
an inheritance that is
not just financial,
but spiritual and moral principles
that I wish to pass on.
Over the years I have written 72 journals
that have most of what God has shown me
through his Word.
My desire is to pass on
some of the most important concepts
I have learned.
As I share my heart
I want them to know
the real me,
what makes me tick
what was valuable in my life

how I love each one of them
so very, very much
and that whereever they go
my love will follow them.

If not me, who?

The more I think about it,
    the more I am convinced
That if not me,
    Who?
If not now
    When?
If not here
    Where?
I may not be able to feed a thousand
    but I can feed one or two at a time.
This world will be saved one or two at a time,
    mostly by insignificant people like you and
    me.
There was a young boy walking along a beach
    throwing back into the ocean
    starfish that would have died
    if not returned to the sea.

A gentleman observed him throwing them back
    one at a time.
He questioned the lad by pointing out that
    there were thousands.
"What difference will you make?" he asked.
The boy responded,
    "I really don't know
    but the ones I throw back
        will know the difference."
This is so true of life.
The people we help, serve, and love
    will know the difference.

You are a masterpiece
Often when change unexpectedly
    comes upon us
    we feel depressed,
        frustrated, and
            confused.
This is when we need
    to remind ourselves
        that "I am a masterpiece."

God made us last and best of all.
As we learn about the human mind,
we begin to realize how amazing we really are.
Computers are wonderful
but they are very
elementary
compared to the brain.
Look in the mirror and see yourself as "a masterpiece."
It will lift your spirit
and help you to see yourself
in a new light.
Your value is immeasurable.

Change takes on many forms

Your little brother dies in a car accident.
You lose your employment due to the company
downsizing.
You car is totaled and you end up spending six
months
in the hospital because of a
reckless driver.
War is declared and the whole economy
goes into a tailspin.
Your sister dies of cancer.
Your house burns down due to a faulty electrical
plug.
I could go on and on with examples of huge
changes
that may impact your life
that are completely outside your control
or ability to influence.

This is when you need to hold on to your faith
and trust God.
Embrace the change.
Take life one day at a time and look for positive ways
to walk through this lonely time.

The greatest change of all

Change is not always bad.
According to God's Word
the greatest change in
all our life is when we
become born again.
When Christ comes into
your life and you repent of all your sins,
you are completely forgiven.
You have a new life
and you can look forward
to living in heaven
throughout all eternity.
There is nothing that compares with this change.
The joy that it brings is unspeakable and full of
glory.
Everything becomes new, and changes in
the way you think

and live
take place over and over again.

Suggestions for living a rich, full life

Live in the now.
Learn from your past.
Plan for your future.
Live one day at a time
Celebrate change.
Don't dwell on your mistakes.
Learn to forgive yourself as well as others.
Don't go to bed angry.
Clarify your dreams.
Learn to be positive.
Organize your time.
Take care of yourself.
Plan your work and work your plan.
Refuse to complain.
Never make excuses.
Be quick to repent.
Realize there is magic in believing.
Stay flexible.
Practice humility.
Walk in the light.

Get plenty of rest.
Have fun.
Laugh.
...?

(Footnotes)
[1] Poem from *Is It Time To Make A Change?* By Deanna Beisser

About the Author

Dr. M. Duane Rawlins is an educator, businessman, speaker, father, and grandfather. He received his doctorate in Education from UCLA and spent 25 years working in the public school system of southern California where his last assignment was as the Assistant Superintendent of schools in Simi Valley. In 1972 he moved to Salem, Oregon with his wife Betty, and their three children, and became President of Rawlins Realty. He has been actively involved with missions and local churches for most of his life. Facing the personal challenges of losing his wife and oldest son to illness has only deepened his desire for intimacy with His Heavenly Father. Thankful for the opportunity to share this message of the Father's heart of love, he travels internationally, bringing hope and healing to many. In 1986, God faithfully provided a new helpmate and wife, Lee Ann, who travels and teaches alongside of Duane. Between them, they have six children and fifteen grandchildren. They reside in Harrisburg, Oregon.

www.ingramcontent.com/pod-product-compliance
Lightning Source LLC
LaVergne TN
LVHW091003080826
845145LV00003B/1111

* 9 7 8 1 9 2 8 7 1 5 3 3 7 *